Briefing Note

Implementing Labour Standards in Construction

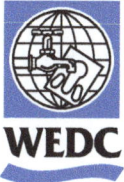

Briefing Note

Implementing Labour Standards in Construction

WEDC

Water, Engineering and Development Centre,
Loughborough University,
Leicestershire, LE11 3TU, UK

© WEDC, Loughborough University, 2003

Ladbury S., Cotton A.P. and Jennings M. (2003)
Implementing Labour Standards in Construction : A sourcebook
WEDC, Loughborough University, UK.

ISBN Paperback: 978 1 84380 092 7
ISBN Ebook: 978 1 78853 303 4
Book DOI: http://dx.doi.org/10.3362/9781788533034

A catalogue record for this book is available from the British Library.

A reference copy of this publication is also available online at:
http://www.lboro.ac.uk/wedc/publications/ilsic.htm

This document is an output from a project funded by the UK Department for International Development (DFID) for the benefit of low-income countries. The views expressed are not necessarily those of DFID. These documents are intended for general usage and readers are advised to use their own discretion when adopting any of the material contained herein and do so at their own risk.

WEDC (The Water, Engineering and Development Centre) at Loughborough University in the UK is one of the world's leading institutions concerned with education, training, research and consultancy for the planning, provision and management of physical infrastructure for development in low- and middleincome countries.

This edition is reprinted and distributed by Practical Action Publishing.
Since 1974, Practical Action Publishing has published and disseminated books and information in support of international development work throughout the world. Practical Action Publishing trades only in support of its parent charity objectives and any profits are covenanted back to Practical Action (Charity Reg. No. 247257, Group VAT Registration No. 880 9924 76).

Implementing Labour Standards in Construction

Lessons from Pilot Studies

What are the labour standards?

Core labour standards

Adopted in 1998, the ILO Declaration on Fundamental Principles and Rights at Work covers 4 *core* labour standards:

1. Freedom of Association and the right to collective bargaining
2. Elimination of forced or compulsory labour
3. Effective abolition of child labour
4. Elimination of discrimination in respect of employment and occupation

These core labour standards apply in all countries that have accepted the ILO Constitution.

'Broader' labour standards

Other *broader* labour standards, based on international conventions of the ILO, include:

5. Health and safety to be addressed
6. Wages to be paid in full and on time
7. Limited working hours and protected overtime pay
8. No repeated casualization (maintaining workers on casual contracts for long periods, to avoid paying standard wages and meeting other legal benefits)
9. Social security regimes applied

These labour standards apply in countries that specifically ratify the appropriate ILO conventions within regional and national law.

*The ILO's Code of Practice considers **HIV/ AIDS** as a workplace issue, to be addressed alongside other labour standards.*

Labour Standards and the Millennium Development Goals

The Millennium Development Goals and associated targets seek to combat extreme poverty and address social and human development in areas of decent employment for youth, discrimination against women, trade and environmental degradation.

These goals and targets can be supported through maximising the contribution of a construction industry that provides infrastructure and services while improving the **quality** and **quantity** of work available to the poor.

A recent DFID-funded research project has sought to improve the labour rights of construction workers through drawing attention to the contribution of labour standards in construction to poverty reduction.

Part of the project has been to disseminate lessons learned and develop influencing agendas, seeking to mainstream the adoption of labour standards in national and international procurement procedures.

http://wedc.Lboro.ac.uk/

WEDC

Why are labour standards important for the construction sector?

- The construction sector is one of the world's largest employers of temporary workers. It provides:
  - 7% of global employment
  - typically 10% of a developing country's GNP

- As a major source of employment for (usually) poor workers, the construction sector is also one of the most dangerous and insecure:

Health and safety

Approximately 100,000 deaths occur on construction sites each year – the equivalent of 1 death every 5 minutes.
Worldwide, construction workers are three times more likely to be killed and twice as likely to be injured as workers in other occupations.

Wages and casual employment

Competition in bidding for work often results in contractors pushing down wages and employing a casual labour force. Temporary workers' wages may not be paid for many months – in some cases up to a year.

Protecting the vulnerable

Many temporary construction workers are unskilled migrants, unaware of their rights. The informal labour market is characterized by some of the most vulnerable groups in society who otherwise do not have a voice.

Labour standards and poverty

Decent employment and working conditions affect people's basic human rights and freedoms, enhance dignity and well-being and help to foster the social and political stability needed for economic growth.

Applied appropriately, labour standards support the livelihoods of workers, reducing their vulnerability – and that of their dependants – to such shocks as work-related illness, injury or redundancy.

Worldwide, an underlying problem is the lack of effective mechanisms to ensure that labour laws are applied and monitored.

Lessons from 3 pilot studies

Between 1998 and 2003, pilot studies funded by the UK's Department for International Development (DFID) were carried out in Ghana, India and Zambia to investigate how to overcome constraints in applying labour standards in different contractual contexts for infrastructure construction.

Small-scale, formal contracting in Ghana – a DFID-funded bridge construction project

- Implementing labour standards requires a consultative process, facilitated by dialogue between client, contractor and workers (in this case through a trade union).
  - Ghanaian contractors were initially reluctant to provide protective clothing, for fear that employees may sell items issued to them.

- Incorporating appropriate clauses into Terms and Conditions of Contract is a key mechanism for ensuring the **implementation** and **monitoring** of labour standards.
  - A clause incorporated in the Ghana project specifies procedures in the event of an accident on site.

- Costs of implementing labour standards need to be incorporated into bills of quantities. Bid evaluations can then provide a "level playing field" for all bidders.
  - Trade Union representatives in Ghana needed costs to support transport to reach remote sites.

- Monitoring the application of labour standards is crucial and requires supporting mechanisms.
  - Monitoring of wage payments in Ghana could only be done when correct employment records were well kept.

- A comprehensive training and awareness programme needs to be part of an integral plan to develop the capacity of contractors.

Community-contracting in India – a local-government funded infrastructure programme

- Liabilities associated with community-contracting are rarely made explicit, but must be understood and mechanisms put in place to protect both the workforce and those responsible.
  - The transfer of responsibility to local government institutions also needs to be accompanied by transfer of liability.
- Strong social relations can be a safeguard for workers (through knowing who they work for), but also used in coercion.
  - Health and safety considerations are a key issue, as pressure can be put on workers not to claim for injury costs from a known community leader.
- Identify what the community can provide. Prioritise what they cannot.
  - In many cases the local community can help to provide water and latrines for workers.

Formal versus informal contracts

Labour standards are normally applied in formal contracts, where there is a clear employment relationship.
Informal, small-scale contracting is more widely practised in the construction industry in many developing countries.
Labour standards should also be applied in conditions of community contracting (where the community, or a section of it, functions as the contractor and is responsible for the implementation of the works) and self-help, voluntary schemes.

Voluntary unpaid labour in Zambia – an international NGO-led water supply and sanitation programme

- Conditions of voluntary unpaid labour need careful consideration. Long-term unpaid work risks undermining livelihoods – inflicting costs, not benefits, on the poor.
  - A construction project required the community, mainly women, to work unpaid for 6-9 months. The community viewed this as preventing them from earning income elsewhere and the use of unpaid labour was stopped.

- A voluntary unpaid approach should only be adopted on a short-term basis, where it is understood and agreed to by all stakeholders.

- Voluntary labourers forego rights to wages and permanent employment, but *all* other labour standards apply.
  - Particular care must be given to ensure equality of treatment, health and safety provision, and protection from child labour.

Information sources

The findings of the studies in Ghana, India and Zambia have been compiled into a publication, providing guidance on the collaborative process and contractual issues for implementing and monitoring labour standards.

Implementing Labour Standards in Construction – A Sourcebook
S Ladbury, A Cotton and M Jennings

WEDC, Loughborough University, 2003

The Sourcebook identifies key steps, with detailed guidance for what to do to make each step operational. It also includes examples of relevant contract clauses and a sample Terms of Reference for carrying out a baseline study.

The **Sourcebook** can be downloaded from the WEDC publications website:
http://wedc.Lboro.ac.uk/publications/index.htm

What people say about the Sourcebook

"I am a great fan of the…handbook…use it constantly and have given it to many others", *Construction Specialist, ILO, Geneva*

"We use a lot of information and references…in the preparation of our proposal reports" *President's Office, Regional Administration and Local Government, Tanzania*

"I've found the sourcebook very useful" *Environmentally and Socially Responsible Procurement, World Bank, Washington*

About this Briefing Note

This Briefing Note provides information on the importance of labour standards to the construction sector. It highlights lessons drawn from 3 pilot studies carried out during a DFID-funded research project 2000 - 2003.

The project was undertaken by WEDC, Loughborough University, in association with the ILO and DFID

ILO
The International Labour Organization (ILO) is a key organization in 'promoting decent work for all', setting standards and creating consensus to sign conventions relating to Labour Standards.
http://www.ilo.org/

DFID
The Department for International Development (DFID) Issues Paper *Labour standards and poverty reduction* published in May 2004, identifies the contribution that well designed and implemented labour standards can make to poverty reduction.
http://www.dfid.gov.uk/

Website

Further details of the research project, including papers and a powerpoint presentation are on the website:
http://wedc.Lboro.ac.uk/projects/new_projects3.php?id=55

This Guidance Note is part of a series covered by ISBN 1 84380 092 6 and was funded by the UK Department for International Development (DFID).
The views expressed, however, are not necessarily those of DFID.

Photographs by Paul Larcher, Brian Reed, Rebecca Scott and Rod Shaw

Published by the
Water, Engineering and Development Centre
Loughborough University UK

WEDC

*People-centred solutions
for sustainable development
since 1971*

For further information, contact:
Rebecca Scott or **Andrew Cotton**

Postal address:
Water, Engineering and Development Centre
Loughborough University
Leicestershire LE11 3TU UK

Email: R.E.Scott@Lboro.ac.uk
                   A.P.Cotton@Lboro.ac.uk
Phone: +44 (0)1509 222885
Fax: +44 (0)1509 211079

Loughborough University

The International Context and National Implications

International Rights and Conventions

The implementation of labour standards is about protecting people, by ensuring that fundamental standards are upheld to provide workers with decent working conditions. It is a principle that is recognized and supported by the highest international bodies, but which needs to be put into practice on site.

> **The Universal Declaration of Human Rights (UDHR)**
>
> Everyone has the right...to just and favourable conditions of work
>
> (From Article 23(1) of the Universal Declaration of Human Rights, adopted and proclaimed by United Nations General Assembly Resolution 217 A (III) of 10 December 1948)

framework for recognizing the rights and dignity of every person. The 191 Member States of the United Nations are pledged to work towards achieving the observance of human rights and fundamental freedoms.

Within the UDHR, Articles 23 and 24 make statements that directly relate to the world of employment:

- *Everyone, without any discrimination, has the right to equal pay for equal work* (Article 23 (2))

- *Everyone who works has the right to just and favourable remuneration...* (Article 23 (3))

- *Everyone has the right to form and to join trade unions* (Article 23 (4))

- *Everyone has the right to rest and leisure, including reasonable limitation of working hours and periodic holidays with pay* (Article 24)

It is with reference to this broad framework of international agreements that UN conventions, and for the most part national laws, operate.

Fundamental Principles and Rights at Work

The International Labour Organization (ILO) was founded in 1919 as the United Nations' specialised agency to promote social justice through internationally recognized labour rights. In its role, the ILO sets minimum standards of labour rights through the formulation of international Conventions and Recommendations.

WEDC

The ILO's *Declaration on Fundamental Principles and Rights at Work* identifies four core areas of labour standards affecting the rights of workers. Seen as rights that enable people to achieve their full potential, they are afforded special status and universal application.

Encapsulated within these four core standards are eight ILO *Conventions* considered by the ILO Governing Body as fundamental to the rights of all people at work, irrespective of the developmental status of individual Member States. A brief summary of the *intention* of each of these conventions is given here.

The four Core Labour Standards

1. Freedom of association and the right to collective bargaining;

2. Elimination of all forms of forced or compulsory labour;

3. Effective abolition of child labour; and

4. Elimination of discrimination in respect of employment and occupation (equality of opportunity and treatment).

Table 1. Core labour standards and associated ILO Conventions

Associated ILO Convention	Intention of the ILO Convention
1. Freedom of association and the right to collective bargaining	
Freedom of Association and Protection of the Right to Organize Convention, 1948 (No.87)	▪ Providing workers the right to join, or establish, organizations of their choosing, without authorization or distinction
Right to Organize and Collective Bargaining Convention, 1949 (No.98)	▪ Protecting workers from acts of anti-union discrimination in respect of their work
2. Elimination of all forms of forced or compulsory labour	
Forced Labour Convention, 1930 (No.29)	▪ Placing an obligation on each member State of the ILO to "suppress the use" of forced or compulsory labour (work demanded from a person under the threat of penalty) at the earliest opportunity
Abolition of Forced Labour Convention, 1957 (No.105)	▪ An extension of the Forced Labour Convention, 1930 to protect workers from being forced to work for reasons of political coercion, education, punishment, economic gain, discipline, or discrimination (racial, social or religious)
3. Effective abolition of child labour	
Minimum Age Convention, 1973 (No.138)	▪ Ensuring that national policies are designed to effectively abolish child labour and raise the minimum age for active engagement in employment to a level appropriate for the development of young people. A child is defined as a person of 14 years or under.
Worst Forms of Child Labour Convention, 1999 (No.182)	▪ Protection of children (in this case persons under the age of 18) from the worst forms of labour, such as slavery, trafficking, armed conflict, and other such work likely to harm the health, safety or moral welfare of children.
4. Elimination of discrimination	
Equal Remuneration Convention, 1951 (No.100)	▪ Ensuring promotion and application of equal remuneration (wage or salary, plus any additional payments in cash or kind) for women and men, for work of equal value (i.e. without discrimination based on sex)
Discrimination (Employment and Occupation) Convention, 1958 (No.111)	▪ Preventing discrimination (exclusion, distinction or preference) within employment and occupational opportunities (including vocational training) on the basis of race, colour, sex, religion, political opinion, national extraction or social origin

Broader, substantive labour standards

While the four Core Labour Standards have universal application, concern for the adoption of a broader range of standards to protect workers has resulted in the recognition of further, more specific, 'substantive' labour standards. These are based on international conventions of the ILO and on provisions contained in regional and national law.

Details of these five substantive Labour Standards and associated ILO Conventions, together with a brief summary of their *intention*, is given in Table 2 overleaf.

> ### The five substantive Labour Standards
>
> 5. Health and safety to be addressed;
>
> 6. Wages to be paid in full and on time, to meet legal minima and be sufficient for basic needs;
>
> 7. Working hours to be limited; overtime to be paid;
>
> 8. No repeated casualization, so employers can avoid paying standard wages or meeting other legal benefits; and
>
> 9. All relevant social security regimes to be applied

National legislation

Member States of the ILO are not legally bound to any of the ILO Conventions they ratify, but by accepting the ILO Constitution they have pledged to respect, promote and work towards the realization of the four Core Labour Standards.

The Conventions therefore provide *benchmarks* that enable nations to debate, adopt and enact legislation and other acts to reflect the provision of the Conventions within their national law.

Of the 178 member States of the ILO (as at March 2005), only 109 have ratified all eight fundamental conventions associated with the core labour standards. A further 26 states have ratified seven fundamental conventions, 13 have ratified six, 10 have ratified five and the rest have ratified four, or less.

The 'substantive' labour standards and associated conventions apply only in countries that specifically ratify the appropriate ILO conventions within national statute law.

The meaning of Conventions and Standards in practice

Converting international Conventions and Standards into national standards that can be applied in practice requires a starting point at the national level. Where Governments have national laws on matters of labour and employment, these are the starting point for developing national standards. Alternatively, industry standards can be used, such as those developed as Collective Agreements between Employers' Associations and respective Trade Unions.

If neither a national law nor Collective Agreement exists, ILO Conventions should be used. However, as the ILO Conventions are not written to be applied to programmes in specific countries, they need to be interpreted for effective application.

What the Core and Substantive Labour Standards mean for the construction sector

Adapted from Ladbury et al (2003) with reference to a pilot programme in Ghana

For labour standards to have a chance of being integrated into bids, proposals and contracts for construction works, their *practical* implications need to be understood. Table 3 (overleaf) provides an indication of some of these practical implications, with reference to the 4 core and 5 substantive labour standards.

The case of HIV/AIDS

In addition to the four core and five substantive labour standards, the ILO has developed a Code of Practice on HIV/AIDS, in recognition that HIV/AIDS is a workplace issue.[1] Practical implications of adopting standards on HIV/AIDS on construction sites may prove to be the most challenging. See Table 4.

---

[1] To access the ILO 'Code of Practice' on HIV/AIDS and a training manual to guide the use of the Code, go to www.ilo.org, click on Social Protection, then The Programme on HIV/AIDS and the World of Work.

Table 2. Substantive labour standards and associated ILO Conventions

Associated ILO Convention	Intention of the ILO Convention
5. Health and safety to be addressed	
Occupational Health and Safety, 1981 (No.155)	▪ Stipulating consultation between employers and workers representatives to formulate, implement and review national policy on occupational safety, occupational health and the work environment; with the intention of preventing accidents or injury to workers in the course of their work and minimizing hazards in the work environment
Safety and Health in Construction, 1988 (No.167)	▪ With particular reference to construction activities; details the responsibilities and actions of employers and workers in ensuring compliance with national health and safety measures in the workplace
6. Wages to be paid in full and on time, to meet legal minima and be sufficient for basic needs	
Minimum Wage Fixing, 1970 (No.131)	▪ Obliging each member State to establish a system of minimum wages, agreed between the authority of that country, workers and employers representatives. Failure to apply the minimum wage to result in appropriate sanctions
Protection of Wages, 1949 (No.95)	▪ Subject to specific exclusions of categories of workers, ensuring that wages are paid in legal tender (with provision of part payment through allowances), not by promissory notes, vouchers or coupons. Payment is to be made direct to the worker, unless otherwise agreed, with the workers free to spend their wages as they wish
Labour Clauses Public Contracts, 1949 (No.94)	▪ Ensuring that contracts in cases where one of the parties to the contract is a public authority and work involves the construction, alteration, repair or demolition of public works include appropriate clauses covering labour conditions to standards set within local trade and industry
7. Working hours to be limited; overtime to be paid	
Weekly Rest (Industry), 1921 (No.14)	▪ Providing workers, subject to identified exclusions, with a rest period of at least 24 consecutive hours in any 7 day work period
Hours of Work (Industry), 1919 (No.1)	▪ Providing workers, subject to identified exclusions (such as shift workers, managers or supervisors, or to carry out urgent works), with a maximum eight hour working day and forty eight hour working week
8. No repeated casualization (whereby workers are engaged for months or years on a series of temporary contracts) so that employers can avoid paying standard wages or meeting other legal benefits such as tax or social security;	
Social Security (Minimum Standard), 1952 (No.102)	▪ Requires the member State to protect specified categories of workers with benefits relating to sickness, unemployment, old-age, employment-injury, maternity, invalidity and the like, subject to specified conditions
Maintenance of Social Security Rights, 1982 (No.157)	▪ With reference to Convention 102 (above) and national legislation, provides for the maintenance of social security payments to workers, in relation to length of employment and other specified factors
9. All relevant social security regimes to be applied	
Conventions are as for 8 above.	

Table 3. Practical implications

Labour standard	Practical implications
Core Labour Standards	
1. Freedom of Association and the right to collective bargaining	Workers should be allowed to establish or join unions, or other work-based organizations and be free not to. These organizations can be used to negotiate working conditions. Contractors should have a co-operative attitude to the workers' trade union representatives, allowing them on to site to talk to workers. Workers may opt to be represented by a local collective or community group, which should be recognized as legitimate negotiating bodies[2].
2. Elimination of all forms of forced or compulsory labour[3]	Forced labour can occur when a contractor forces workers to do overtime or a 7 day week without their consent and under threat of penalty, e.g. job loss.
3. Effective abolition of child labour	Child labour can occur if women bring their children to site and they 'help' with a particular activity, e.g. breaking stones. If stopping this practice prevents women from working, dialogue is vital. Alternative actions, such as providing child care arrangements, may be needed to ensure that women do not lose their jobs.
4. Elimination of discrimination in respect of employment and occupation	Discrimination may be justified in terms of culture, e.g. 'our women like to carry concrete' implying they will not be considered for other jobs. Such attitudes are discriminatory if they limit employment opportunities for a particular group.
Substantive Labour Standards	
5. Health and safety to be addressed	Workplaces must be safe and without risk of injury to employees. National labour law will normally state minimum requirements for protective clothing and safety precautions specific to the industry. The contractor should also undertake obligations to train safety officers and first aiders (with a properly equipped first aid box). Provision of potable water, latrines on site and emergency procedures in the event of an accident may also be prescribed in law. Where the law does not provide an adequate standard, the Collective Agreement between the Employers' Association and Trade Union is the best point of reference.
6. Wages to be paid in full and on time, to meet legal minima and be sufficient for basic needs	The current national minimum wage can be used as a standard, although high inflation may make this out of date. In this case the rate agreed in a Collective Agreement should be applied. If there is no such agreement, the rate used by a local construction company known for good practice is an alternative reference point. Wages should be paid in cash, not in kind.
7. Working hours to be limited; overtime to be paid	National law will specify the 'working week'. Overtime should be paid above this rate according to the national legal formula. Regulations should ensure that the use of task-based/piece work does not lead to self-exploitation and workers having to work longer hours than specified in the legislation.
8. No repeated casualization to avoid meeting wages and other legal benefits[4]	The worker, called a 'casual' but more accurately a 'temporary' worker, is typically paid less than permanent workers and ends up with no pension rights, or access to other benefits such as employment-injury pay.
9. All relevant social security regimes to be applied	All countries have laws regarding registration for social security and these should be followed. If the law does not allow for temporary workers to receive social security, it may be necessary to review, with regulators, how to make regulations on social protection relevant and feasible for all workers.

[2] In many rural areas, there is no trade union representation but workers may form a collective group to enhance their bargaining power. It is important that these local negotiating bodies are recognized.

[3] There is a connection between forced labour and payment in full and on time (points 2 and 6). Failure to pay on time is common and well documented in some countries (e.g. India, Nepal). It results in workers having to borrow from the labour agents or contractors who employ them. Indebtedness in turn creates obligations and the workers can become, in effect 'bonded' to their employer; a situation which can lead to forced labour.

[4] Informal (verbal), short term contracts, without benefits, are the norm in the construction industry in many countries. Standard number 8 seeks to make a distinction between the true casual worker (hired on a daily basis for a short period) and a temporary worker (hired more or less continually by the same employer for months or years) who is treated as a casual, i.e. with none of the benefits of formal employment. Employers should 'move' this group of temporary workers into the permanent worker category.

Table 4. The case of HIV/AIDS	
"Labour standard"	**Practical implications**
10. HIV/AIDS to be addressed	The ILO Code of Practice goes beyond awareness raising to include non-discrimination, confidentiality, care and support. UNAIDS and other agencies produce guidelines for employer good practice with regard to HIV/AIDS. The ideal is to follow the national policy on AIDS if this has been developed. In an example from Ghana, the Ministry of Roads and Transport applied for funding from the Ghana AIDS Commission to mount an education campaign for contractors, workers and communities. Contractors were to allow health staff to visit sites and inform workers about the risks of HIV/AIDS, with workers paid for time spent on HIV/AIDS awareness.

The role of procurement

Worldwide, the construction sector typically provides 10% of a developing country's GNP. International financial institutions (IFIs), multi-lateral and bi-lateral donors are influential in the economy of these countries through procurement contracts in the construction sector.

While governments hold ultimate responsibility in matters of compliance with national law, the policies, procedures and guidelines of procurement contracts affect the degree to which labour standards are incorporated into contract documents, and how much attention is therefore paid to their implementation.

Experience of incorporating labour clauses in procurement documents is limited, but the potential to be had from awareness-raising and moving towards the implementation of labour standards is significant. It is the responsibility of procurement agencies to use their policies and associated activities to leverage the alignment of business opportunities with livelihoods security, social protection and broader poverty reduction. This should start at the early planning stages, with labour standards integrated into procurement guidelines, loan agreements, operational manuals, policy, procedures, directives and other appropriate documentation.

The capacity of government agencies to uphold the law in practice is often limited, especially in situations where the construction sector is characterized by the involvement of numerous small and semi-formal firms through sub-contracting by main contractors. Procurement agencies can also support governments and private sector institutions through capacity building, to enable the effective monitoring and enforcement of labour standards.

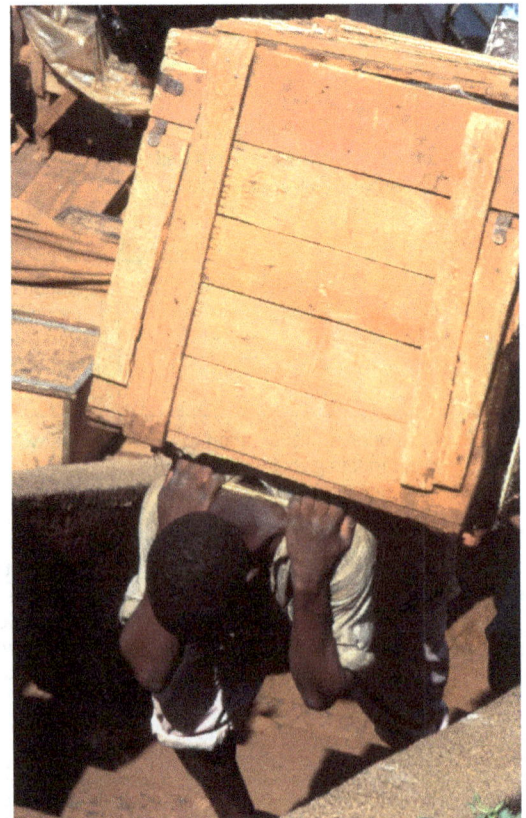

Information sources

Ladbury, S., Cotton, A. and Jennings, M. (2003), *Implementing Labour Standards in Construction A sourcebook*, WEDC, Loughborough University
Available to download from
http://wedc.Lboro.ac.uk/publications/index.htm

Full text of the UDHR
http://www.un.org/Overview/rights.html

About the ILO
http://www.ilo.org/public/english/about/index.htm

The full text of all International Labour Standards can be found on the ILO website from
http://www.ilo.org/ilolex/english/convdisp2.htm (as at April 2005)

Recommendations and guidelines for the role of World Bank procurement in supporting the adoption of international labour standards, including the wording of recommended clauses for inclusion in standard bidding documents, are contained in the following report:

IFBWW, (2004), *Improving Working and Living Conditions in Construction: Addressing Needs Through International Labour Standards in World Bank Procurement*; Draft Recommendations and Technical Guidance from the International Federation of Building and Wood Workers, March 2004.

The report is available to download from
http://www.ifbww.org/files/Improving_Working_and_84E5F.pdf

About this Guidance Note

This note provides an overview of the place of labour standards in international and national frameworks, conventions and agreements.

It forms part of a series of publications on Implementing Labour Standards in Construction:

A Sourcebook
Briefing Note   : Lessons from Pilot Studies
Guidance Note 1 : The International Context and National Implications
Guidance Note 2 : Making Labour Standards Operational
Guidance Note 3 : Including Labour Standards in the Contract

These are all based on a review of international literature together with lessons learned from pilot studies carried out in Ghana, India and Zambia during a DFID-funded research project.

The project was undertaken by WEDC, Loughborough University, in association with the ILO and DFID

ILO

The International Labour Organization (ILO) is a key organization in "promoting decent work for all", setting standards and creating consensus to sign conventions relating to Labour Standards.
http://www.ilo.org/

DFID

The Department for International Development (DFID) issues paper "Labour standards and poverty reduction" published in May 2004, identifies the contribution that well designed and implemented labour standards can make to poverty reduction.
http://www.dfid.gov.uk/

Website

Further details of the research project, including the Sourcebook, briefing note, guidance notes, papers and powerpoint presentation are available to view and download on the WEDC website:
http://wedc.Lboro.ac.uk/projects/new_projects3.php?id=55

This Guidance Note is part of a series covered by ISBN 1 84380 092 6 and was funded by the UK Department for International Development (DFID).
The views expressed, however, are not necessarily those of DFID.

Photographs by Rod Shaw

Published by the
Water, Engineering and Development Centre
Loughborough University UK

WEDC

*People-centred solutions
for sustainable development
since 1971*

For further information, contact:
Rebecca Scott or **Andrew Cotton**

Postal address:
Water, Engineering and Development Centre
Loughborough University
Leicestershire LE11 3TU UK

Email: R.E.Scott@Lboro.ac.uk
              A.P. Cotton@Lboro.ac.uk
Phone: +44 (0)1509 222885
Fax: +44 (0)1509 211079

Loughborough University

Making Labour Standards Operational

This guidance note introduces an approach to making labour standards operational in construction contracts. It introduces the reader to a strategy: starting with identifying the gaps between law and practice and moving through to monitoring the application of labour standards on site. It concludes with suggestions on how to scale-up the approach for broader application.

A fuller description of this approach can be found in *Implementing Labour Standards in Construction – A Sourcebook*. See the Reference section for details.

A key stage in the approach is to develop appropriate contract clauses, include and cost them in the Contract and Bill of Quantities. Details of this stage are given in the accompanying Guidance Note 3: Including Labour Standards in the Contract.

From adoption to application

Worldwide, an underlying problem is not the lack of labour law as such, but the lack of effective means to ensure that labour laws are applied and monitored. Ways are needed to help ensure that labour standards are not only adopted but also applied, especially in circumstances where limited resources and poor monitoring make their application less likely.

Firstly, it is important that all parties involved in the implementation of labour standards are involved in setting the standards. Collaboration should bring together all relevant stakeholders, including the employer, the contractor and their workforce, to identify *how* to implement and monitor labour standards. With stakeholders involved, they will understand what is going on and can voice their concerns, so are far more likely to co-operate as the process continues.

A collaborative process should be initiated to:

1. identify gaps between law and practice;

2. bring key stakeholders together to determine roles and responsibilities; and

3. decide which standards to focus on.

Steps 2 and 3 are particularly influenced by whether the contracting procedure is to be a formal or informal. The implications of formal and informal contracting are highlighted at these points in the process.

Following on from these first steps, the same group of stakeholders should agree on procedures for implementing and monitoring compliance with appropriate labour standards. These steps are common to both formal and informal contracting procedures.

WEDC

The steps recommended to continue this process are:

4. develop appropriate clauses, write them into the Contract document and cost them into the bill of quantities *(see box below)*;

5. allow for pre-bid and award of contract consultation;

6. develop a way to inform workers of their rights;

7. incorporate incentives and/or sanctions for the contractor;

8. enable key stakeholders to discuss progress together; and

9. agree how monitoring will be carried out on site.

Developing contract clauses

While responsibility for adhering to the contract clauses lies formally with the contractor, the *process* of developing appropriate clauses is best achieved through consultation with employers, contractors, community groups and labourers alike.

Guidance Note 3: Including Labour Standards in the Contract, goes into more detail about how to develop appropriate Contract clauses, include and cost these into the Contract documents.

The steps are described in more detail here.

1. Identify gaps between law and practice

While labour standards may have a legal or policy basis in a given country, there are likely to be gaps in their adoption when it comes to standard Contract documents, agreements (for example Collective Agreements between Trade Unions and Employers' Representatives) and site practice. It is important therefore to first review where the gaps currently lie, to identify which standards need to be focused on for application. The review can be supported through addressing a series of questions.

Examples of the *type* and *range* of questions to be asked are given in Table 1.

2. Determine roles and responsibilities of key stakeholders

The full range of key stakeholders (primary and secondary) who have a role and responsibility towards the implementation of labour standards should be identified.

Possible key stakeholders

At the *project* level key stakeholders will typically include:

- the labourers (men and women, skilled and unskilled);
- the client (such as local government, or an NGO); and
- the contractor / sub-contractors (that is, the implementing group).

At *national* and *sub-national* level key stakeholders could include:

- government bodies;
- employers' representatives;
- Trade Unions and other workers' representatives;
- community associations;
- the research community;
- NGOs; and
- Donors.

Having identified the relevant stakeholders, it is important to determine the interests of each of them at the outset. Through a process of consultation and with the help of an experienced facilitator, the following steps should be taken:

i. Determine the parties to the contractual relationship and identify who is liable for what;

ii. Clarify the roles and responsibilities, with regard to implementing labour standards, for each stakeholder; and

iii. Identify ways to inform workers about labour standards and what new site practices are proposed.

Implications for roles and responsibilities of formal and informal contracts

Different forms of contract are used within the construction sector for minor works in low- and middle-income countries, namely;

- conventional (formal) contracts and
- community-contracting or voluntary free-labour (informal) contracts

Conventional (formal) contracting is used in the procurement of infrastructure where contracts are awarded through competitive tender. Such procedures typically involve an Employer, Engineer and Contractor(s).

For example: a government department lets a construction contract to a private sector contractor.

- the Government is the Employer, having planned and designed the work and being responsible for paying for its completion.

- the Government appoints an Engineer to represent their interests as the work progresses;

- in accordance with procedures, a Contractor is appointed, through a competitive bidding process, to carry out the construction work.

Table 1. Examples of the type and range of questions to help identify gaps		
Area being considered	**Example questions**	**Comments**
National law and policy	- What national or sectoral commitments are made regarding the use of child labour? - Is the law on minimum wages up to date?	It is a good idea to contact the ILO Office in the country, the Ministry of Labour and the national Trade Union Congress, to get copies of relevant labour laws and Collective Agreements.
Standard Contract documents	- Do standard or specific clauses make reference to the adoption of labour standards? - Who is responsible, and what capacity is there, for monitoring?	A crucial issue is to determine whether the contract clauses, contained in the key contract documents used for the procurement of works, are inadequate regarding provision of labour standards, or whether the standards are there but are not being monitored or enforced. In cases of *informal contracting*, the situation is less clear. In the absence of formal contracts, it is important to identify where awareness and promotion of standards is needed to protect all parties, especially in relation to health and safety measures.
Collective Agreements between Trade Unions and Employers	- Is there disparity between labour standards in the Agreements and in national law? Can gaps in legislation be filled? - What proportion of the labour force are unionized and where are they located?	It is important to engage all relevant Trade Unions/worker representatives and Employers' Associations in discussions at the earliest stage possible. It is then possible to identify their interest and role in becoming part of the wider stakeholder group at a later stage.
Site practice	- Are labour standards that may be legally binding or agreed carried out in practice? - What is the attitude of contractors to unions?	If information relating to current site practice is not already available, a systematic, simple baseline survey should be carried out. This can be in the form of a short questionnaire, supplemented by informal interviews with client groups, implementers, workers and site agents. It should identify the scale of main issues to be addressed. Where possible, the baseline survey should be designed and carried out by technical staff, to help foster a sense of responsibility with those who may otherwise dismiss the matter as being for social scientists. They will also then be better placed to design effective solutions to improve and monitor the application of labour standards.

However, many minor works contracts in low- and middle-income countries are procured on the basis of *informal contracts*: community contracting or voluntary free-labour contracts.

In *community contracting*, the role of the contractor is taken on by a community, or group of individuals, who become responsible for implementation of the works and are paid for their labour. Such groups are generally not registered and do not normally bid for work as would happen for conventional contracts.

When work is implemented at the community level (the informal sector) the legal and regulatory framework is less clear. Community contracts are usually based on less formal agreements, which can include verbal agreements. It is essential that the role played by each party in the contract is made clear in relation to the responsibility for implementing and monitoring the protection of workers' rights. It may be necessary for a party to the contract, such as a Community-Based Organization, to be legally registered. If they are to become legally responsible for worker protection, the CBO must first be aware of the obligations and liabilities this will entail (for example their responsibility towards the safety of workers) and have suitable legal protection to be able to honour these.

Even if national labour legislation and regulatory frameworks provide comprehensive protection for formally employed workers (although they may still be poorly implemented and monitored), they are unlikely to do so for community contracting. Workers may not be protected under 'labour law' as such, but rather under laws relating to welfare or social security. It is important that all parties understand their obligations, duties and rights in such cases.

Voluntary free-labour schemes are a style adopted by many NGOs, bi- and multi-lateral agencies in community infrastructure development programmes. Free labour is seen as a way in which the community can contribute to the scheme, promoting a sense of 'ownership' and so ensuring that needs are met, while cost-sharing and capacity for community-managed maintenance is developed.

In such situations, strong social relationships between those managing construction works (often influential people from the community) and the community-based labourers can affect how well labour standards are adhered to. Elements of coercion and social pressure can arise so that, for example, a marginalised member of the community does not feel able to claim for injury-related costs from an influential community leader.

National labour law is unlikely to cover unpaid work. Workers should understand that, while they agree to carry out unpaid work, they do not forfeit their entitlement to other rights. The nature of the unpaid work, its complexity, frequency and duration should be openly discussed with communities, to enable them to accept the work on agreed terms.

In the case of community contracting, a key issue is the **transfer of liability** from a regulated institution to an informal (community) structure. The community structure may not be aware of their liability and how best to protect both themselves and the workforce. Unless consultation is carried out with all relevant stakeholders, in such circumstances *assumed* and *actual* liability are likely to be very different.

Paid or unpaid labour?

A series of questions can guide the decision on whether to use voluntary free-labour. These include:

- What is the scale and frequency of the work? Work that is going to take place over the long-term or requires repeat work should be paid.

- How complex and safe are the tasks? Risky tasks require skilled paid workers.

- What standard of work is to be achieved? Can this be achieved by unskilled workers?

- How will carrying out voluntary work affect people's ability to earn a living?

- What is the objective of adopting a voluntary labour approach? Is it to enable a sense of community ownership, to create structure for long term development, or to save costs?

If the answers to these and other questions (more are provided in Ladbury et al, 2003, pp.18-19) suggest that the community is being offered an unfair deal, paid work should be the norm.

In the absence of an alternative to voluntary work, community leaders, those who will supervise the work and the workers themselves should all be aware of, and support the need for, applying labour standards.

3. Decide which standards to focus on

It is the case that not all nine labour standards (four core and five substantive standards) can be addressed adequately or equally in every situation. Limited capacity, finances, time, knowledge, or commitment may result in a need to focus on the key labour standard issues identified from surveys of current site practice. This will be particularly relevant in the case of informal contracting.

The interpretation of certain labour standards within national law may be difficult, to the extent that it takes too many resources to address them. This may be particularly relevant in the case of community contracting, where compliance with all nine labour standards can be too much of a burden for the community to manage. In practice, it may be necessary to focus on the standards identified and prioritised by the community themselves, either through local measures, or with appropriate assistance.

Table 2 gives an overview of issues that may arise when identifying which standards to focus on, as well as providing suggestions of possible actions to take during implementation. It relates primarily to the case of community contracting and voluntary free-labour (i.e. informal) schemes.

The stakeholder responsible for taking specific action is not clearly defined. In some schemes, certain actions will be the responsibility of local government, while others are the responsibility of NGOs or community organizations who have taken on the role of the Employer.

Agreement as to which standards to focus on should be reached with all key stakeholders through open consultation. Everyone will then know both the current situation and what the goals are. While certain standards may warrant greater focus and commitments of time and resources, ideally there should be a long-term commitment to addressing all nine standards in due course.

Particular issues for temporary and unpaid workers

In cases of unpaid work, workers have "forgone" their rights to labour standards applying to wages and deliberate casualization. However, due to the vulnerability of workers in such cases, most other labour standards should be reviewed, particularly those relating to:

- health and safety measures,
- no forced labour,
- agreements on working hours,
- equality of treatment, and
- no child labour.

We now consider the remaining steps in the process. These are relevant to both formal and informal contracting procedures.

4. Develop appropriate clauses, include and cost them into the Contract documents

This stage is described in detail in the accompanying *Guidance Note 3: Including Labour Standards in the Contract.* The Guidance Note considers how to develop contract clauses, provides examples of relevant contract and specification clauses developed in Ghana and India, and identifies costs and benefits associated with applying labour standards.

5. Carry out pre-bid and award of contract meetings

Few small-scale contractors in developing countries have direct experience of being responsible for implementing labour standards on site. Potential bidders need to be provided with relevant information, so that they understand what is expected of them and know how to budget for each standard specified.

- Pilot studies have shown that briefings on how to cost labour standards and how to maintain employment records for monitoring purposes are essential. Ideally two briefings are necessary: one before bids are prepared and one on the award of contract.

Table 2. Issues arising and action to take in the case of community contracting and voluntary free-labour schemes

Labour Standard	The issues	Actions: What can be done?
1. Freedom of Association and the right to collective bargaining.	Trade unions are usually not active in the informal sector, or found on many rural community contracting sites.	■ Recognize local informal groups that represent workers e.g. CBOs, NGOs, workers groups, who can develop home-grown solutions.
2. The elimination of all forms of forced or compulsory labour.	In some schemes, infrastructure can be denied unless labour is provided on an unpaid basis.	■ Check that the agreement to provide unpaid labour is acceptable to the community at large, not just the leaders; ■ Ensure that there are exemptions for those deemed to be vulnerable, e.g. pregnant women, the elderly, children of school-going age, the disabled, poorer and female-headed households.
3. The effective abolition of child labour (under 15 years, or the country-accepted minimum legal age applicable to the type of work).	In poorest households or child-headed households, children may be obliged to work.	■ Discuss options with parents/children (some may be child-headed households); ■ Review whether work interferes with children's education & restructure tasks and working times to suit; ■ Set priorities and establish an action plan towards eliminating child labour, without increasing poverty.
4. The elimination of discrimination in respect of employment and occupation.	Gender wage disparities may be endemic & institutionalized. Lack of opportunities for women & casual workers to become skilled construction workers reinforces unequal wages. Typically, there exists in-built bias against creating viable jobs for women or disabled workers in paid work.	■ Specify equal wages in contract rates; ■ Provide training to raise awareness among contractors/foremen; ■ Use women's groups or networks to work with women; ■ Try rotating roles among men and women; ■ Build in skills training for women in aspects of engineering, supervision, etc.; ■ Allocate tasks to groups of women who can organize the work amongst themselves, to fit in with other responsibilities.
5. Health and Safety to be assured.	*Accident prevention* Community/self-help groups or small contractors are not familiar with safety standards and labourers are primarily local unskilled workers. *Dealing with accidents* Typically there is no liability coverage, so victims have to pay their own medical expenses and cover any income loss.	■ Develop a specific health and safety proposal at the design stage, which identifies potential hazards and risks and how they will be dealt with; e.g. only skilled workers permitted to carry out risky tasks; ■ Prioritize accident prevention through awareness creation and training. Focus on the concept of removing hazards and risk as a first step. Provide protective clothing and first aid kits on site; ■ Provide awareness training on risks. Make provision for insurance/worker's compensation & availability of first aid kits in project costs. Where possible, use health and safety competence as a criteria for choosing contractors. ■ Distinguish between minor & serious accidents: - minor accidents require an immediate response to cover medical treatment costs and loss of income; - serious accidents need additional provisions such as insurance against death, physical disablement.

Table 2. Issues arising and action to take in the case of community contracting and voluntary free-labour schemes ...*continued*

Labour Standard	The issues	Actions: What can be done?
5. *Health and Safety to be assured (continued)*	*Protective clothing* Low awareness of the need. Costs high relative to wages.	▪ Create awareness of its importance; Include costs for necessary clothing as a prime cost item in the Contract.
	First Aid Lack of awareness and limited understanding of responsibilities	▪ Decide with the client & community on storage, maintenance and ownership of first aid equipment; ▪ Establish a safety committee & emergency procedures. Nominate and train a safety officer & first aid person. Promote health education and HIV/AIDS awareness & prevention.
	Amenities (drinking water, sanitation, food) Scale of works often too small to warrant the formal provision of drinking water and sanitation.	▪ Include drinking water & sanitation facilities as a prime cost item if they cannot be accessed from neighbouring households (for local workers); ▪ Food may be provided by community members but if not encourage food sellers on to sites.
6. Wages to be paid in full and on time, to meet legal minima, and be sufficient for basic needs.	Wages are often set low because of a surplus of labour, resulting in difficulties for workers to support themselves. Minimum wages are often well below market rates. Wages paid late, as the client does not pay on time, so the contractor has no cash flow.	▪ Assess minimum wage to see its relevance; ▪ Set a realistic wage for casual and permanent workers that supports people's livelihoods, i.e. provide a *living wage;* ▪ Be transparent in setting wage rates. Keep a register of payments and provide wage slips; ▪ Develop means to maximise paying wages on time – poor people cannot extend credit lines.
7. Working hours to be limited; overtime to be paid.	Workers can be obliged to work long hours, especially if the contract includes a penalty clause for delays. In self-help schemes, workers may have little influence over how long they work. The requirement to do additional work may conflict with other livelihood strategies.	▪ Keep work records and monitor *with the worker.* ▪ Create additional jobs, rather than increasing the workload of existing workers. ▪ Set task rates with reasonable time scales. ▪ Review the management and supervision of works. ▪ Discuss with the community and workers the scheduling of work such that it facilitates workers' other responsibilities.
8. No repeated casualization to avoid meeting wages & other legal benefits	Casual workers not treated equally because they are usually unskilled – wages lower and no social security.	▪ Pay a wage at least equivalent to the minimum wage, or the market rate for similar work, whichever is higher; ▪ In the absence of other safety nets, prioritize accident insurance.
9. All relevant social security regimes to be applied.	Difficulties in bringing irregular casual workers into social security nets/accident insurance. Community groups do not have accident coverage or other social security provision.	▪ Explore possible coverage under existing social security schemes. If casual workers cannot be covered an accident insurance scheme will be necessary, especially for serious accidents. ▪ Make provision within the project (at local level) to deal with minor accidents quickly, e.g. create a fund which can be used to support costs for treatment, transport, etc.

6. Develop a way to ensure that workers are informed of their rights

The issue of labour standards may be new to workers as well as the contractor. Workers and communities need to be made aware of what their rights and entitlements are, and why they are important. Responsibility for awareness raising should be agreed and an awareness-raising plan worked out together with stakeholders, including the workers themselves.

Steps for putting the awareness-raising plan into action include:

i.   Get representatives of stakeholder groups (trade unions, government department of social security or health, etc.) to visit communities/sites. Where relevant bodies are not available, individuals equipped with the relevant basic information can carry out these tasks;

ii. Use visual examples to explain standards. For example, if protective clothing is to be provided, take examples of each item. If records are to be kept, take the record forms;

iii. Anticipate initial problems. For example, in Ghana the cost of a pair of safety boots is equivalent to a month's wage so the inclination to sell them at times of emergency is strong. A good consultative relationship between workers and contractors (or site representatives and foremen) enables these issues to be discussed and resolved at a site level; and

iv. Have labour standards as a standard item on the agenda of the regular site meeting, with a worker representative present who can discuss any labour standards issues from the workers' point of view.

7. Develop incentives and/or sanctions for the contractors

Contractors respond well to incentives – such as a bonus paid when labour standards are deemed to have improved, or payment on completion if compliance with all labour standards has been achieved.

In informal contracting, social pressure may be the major incentive. Loss of social or political status for those with responsibilities can be a strong incentive for compliance.

Sanctions may also work, particularly in the case of repeated non-compliance by a contractor. In such instances they can be in the form of disqualification from bidding for future contracts, withholding payment, or social pressure through open discussion at site meetings.

A combination of incentives and sanctions might prove most appropriate. To ensure that labour standards can be applied without raising accusations of unfairness, the criteria for compliance need to be clearly identified and contractors fully informed of their implications, prior to the bidding process.

8. Bring key stakeholders together to discuss progress

Ongoing dialogue between key stakeholders provides a forum to discuss both progress and difficulties encountered in the implementation of labour standards. Regular workshops can involve the client, contractors, trade unions, workers, government and other interested parties. These may be held every 3-6 months for the first year or so, then annually as work continues.

Such workshops should allow for an honest exchange of views, where all stakeholders can openly discuss ways to overcome any challenges being faced.

9. Establish how monitoring will be carried out on site

Labour standards are generally not implemented because they are not monitored. Without the application of incentives and / or sanctions, contractors are unlikely to see the need or benefit in implementing required standards.

Monitoring should occur both within the workplace (i.e. on site) and by an independent body, such as a trade union, as part of an agreed process. Robust monitoring mechanisms are required that check on implementation. These can include:

- *visual monitoring*, e.g. to check on correct use of protective clothing and equipment, that women are not restricted to certain types of work, etc.;

- viewing the *record systems*, to check on working hours, pay, accidents and so on; and

- *discussions with workers*, to cross check the recorded and viewed information.

Regular site meetings should be held and used as a forum to discuss and address issues arising from the monitoring process.

In a pilot study in Ghana, the contractors first needed a system for recording who was employed, for how long, on what task, and on what pay. Without a recording system, monitoring was not possible. The accuracy of the records needed to be checked by talking with the workers, so visits to site were carried out by an independent body (an NGO).

Scaling-up the experience

Once strong systems of implementation and monitoring have been established in pilot studies, they can be considered for wider application. Scaling-up to the construction sector as a whole requires a well thought out plan of action.

The experience from the pilot studies carried out first needs to be in a replicable form. Establish:

- well documented, easy to reproduce, *briefing notes* for contractors and *training materials* for engineers and those who will monitor the application of standards;

- agreed *responsibilities* for training, briefing and awareness raising; and

- a well established *monitoring system* (with standard recording sheets, if required)

From this, develop a *strategy* for scaling-up.

- Start the strategy based on who you know and work with, then bring in other stakeholders as appropriate;

- Initially target programmes in locations where engineers and contractors are familiar with labour standards;

- Introduce labour standards into the bid assessment criteria, as well as in guidance on procurement procedures; and

- Develop links with ministries and agencies interested in specific labour standards, such as child labour, or gender equity.

The outline of a five-step strategy for institutionalizing labour standards in the construction sector was developed in Ghana, from experience of a pilot study within the Department of Feeder Roads, Ministry of Roads and Transport. It is indicated in the table below (adapted from Ladbury *et al*, 2003, p.59)

The strategy for scaling-up will hopefully lead to national level consultation on the contribution of labour standards to broader issues such as poverty reduction and security of livelihoods.

Table 3. Scaling-up labour standards in Ghana: the proposed outline strategy

Step 1. Implement labour standards on the donor-assisted *Bridges programme:* This donor-funded scheme involved very minor works in 2 regions of Ghana. It allowed all systems to be piloted for transfer and adaptation elsewhere.

Step 2. Implement on the donor-assisted *Feeder Roads programme:* This donor-funded programme involved more substantial works, using a higher category of contractor in more regions of the country. It also involved a higher degree of contractor and site engineer training.

Step 3. Implement on all *Department of Feeder Roads (DFR) programmes* in Ghana. This involved influencing other donors who support DFR to include labour standards implementation in their processes and budgets.

Step 4. Implement on all *Ministry of Roads and Transport programmes:* This step involved government-funded projects and meant extending labour standards to DFR's sister departments, such as Urban Roads and Highways. While these are outside DFR's jurisdiction, they are within its sphere of influence. By this time, a number of contractors and engineers would be trained.

Step 5. Implement throughout Ghana: Starting with other line departments carrying out infrastructure work (e.g. Ministry of Works and Housing, Education, etc.) this would be supported by other ministries interested in specific standards (e.g. Women's Affairs, Poverty Reduction).

Note: The DFR had 'control' over what happened only with programmes it was responsible for implementing (steps 1, 2 and 3). It could however influence decision makers in other ministries (steps 4 and 5) directly and by building up a constituency of others who were supportive of labour standards.

Information sources

Ladbury, S. (2001), *The Social Aspects of Construction Study (SAC),* Briefing Paper, February 2001, unpublished

Ladbury, S., (2003), *Progress and constraints on labour standards in Ghana. Is the scope too broad – or is it adequate in the Ghana context?,* unpublished

Ladbury, S., Cotton, A. and Jennings, M. (2003), *Implementing Labour Standards in Construction – A sourcebook*, WEDC, Loughborough University
Available to download from:
http://wedc.Lboro.ac.uk/publications/index.htm

Scott, R. and Cotton, A. (2004), *Implementing Labour Standards in Construction*, in ILO (2004), Labour Based Technology: A review of current practice (2003/2004), Volume 2: Papers of the 10th Regional Seminar, International Labour Organization (ILO), Switzerland

About this Guidance Note

This note introduces an approach to making labour standards operational in infrastructure works.

It forms part of a series of publications on Implementing Labour Standards in Construction:

> A Sourcebook
> Briefing Note   :   Lessons from Pilot Studies
> Guidance Note 1 :   The International Context and National Implications
> Guidance Note 2 :   Making Labour Standards Operational
> Guidance Note 3 :   Including Labour Standards in the Contract

These are all based on a review of international literature together with lessons learned from pilot studies carried out in Ghana, India and Zambia during a DFID-funded research project.

The project was undertaken by WEDC, Loughborough University, in association with the ILO and DFID

ILO

The International Labour Organization (ILO) is a key organization in "promoting decent work for all", setting standards and creating consensus to sign conventions relating to Labour Standards.
http://www.ilo.org/

DFID

The Department for International Development (DFID) issues paper "Labour standards and poverty reduction" published in May 2004, identifies the contribution that well designed and implemented labour standards can make to poverty reduction.
http://www.dfid.gov.uk/

Website

Further details of the research project, including the Sourcebook, briefing note, guidance notes, papers and powerpoint presentation are available to view and download on the WEDC website:
http://wedc.Lboro.ac.uk/projects/new_projects3.php?id=55

This Guidance Note is part of a series covered by ISBN 1 84380 092 6 and was funded by the UK Department for International Development (DFID).
The views expressed, however, are not necessarily those of DFID.

Photographs by Rebecca Scott and Rod Shaw

Published by the
Water, Engineering and Development Centre
Loughborough University UK

People-centred solutions
for sustainable development
since 1971

For further information, contact:
Rebecca Scott or **Andrew Cotton**

Postal address:
Water, Engineering and Development Centre
Loughborough University
Leicestershire LE11 3TU UK

Email: R.E.Scott@Lboro.ac.uk
           A.P. Cotton@Lboro.ac.uk
Phone: +44 (0)1509 222885
Fax: +44 (0)1509 211079

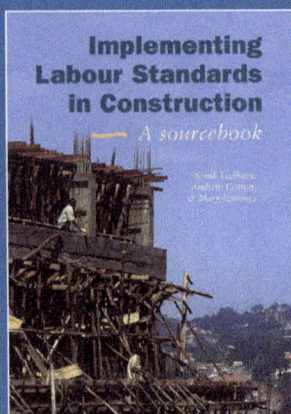

Loughborough University

Information sources

Ladbury, S. (2001), *The Social Aspects of Construction Study (SAC),* Briefing Paper, February 2001, unpublished

Ladbury, S., (2003), *Progress and constraints on labour standards in Ghana. Is the scope too broad – or is it adequate in the Ghana context?,* unpublished

Ladbury, S., Cotton, A. and Jennings, M. (2003), *Implementing Labour Standards in Construction – A sourcebook*, WEDC, Loughborough University
Available to download from:
http://wedc.Lboro.ac.uk/publications/index.htm

Scott, R. and Cotton, A. (2004), *Implementing Labour Standards in Construction*, in ILO (2004), Labour Based Technology: A review of current practice (2003/2004), Volume 2: Papers of the 10th Regional Seminar, International Labour Organization (ILO), Switzerland

About this Guidance Note

This note introduces an approach to making labour standards operational in infrastructure works.

It forms part of a series of publications on Implementing Labour Standards in Construction:

> *A Sourcebook*
> *Briefing Note*   :   *Lessons from Pilot Studies*
> *Guidance Note 1*   :   *The International Context and National Implications*
> *Guidance Note 2*   :   *Making Labour Standards Operational*
> *Guidance Note 3*   :   *Including Labour Standards in the Contract*

These are all based on a review of international literature together with lessons learned from pilot studies carried out in Ghana, India and Zambia during a DFID-funded research project.

The project was undertaken by WEDC, Loughborough University, in association with the ILO and DFID

ILO

The International Labour Organization (ILO) is a key organization in "promoting decent work for all", setting standards and creating consensus to sign conventions relating to Labour Standards.
http://www.ilo.org/

DFID

The Department for International Development (DFID) issues paper "Labour standards and poverty reduction" published in May 2004, identifies the contribution that well designed and implemented labour standards can make to poverty reduction.
http://www.dfid.gov.uk/

Website

Further details of the research project, including the Sourcebook, briefing note, guidance notes, papers and powerpoint presentation are available to view and download on the WEDC website:
http://wedc.Lboro.ac.uk/projects/new_projects3.php?id=55

This Guidance Note is part of a series covered by ISBN 1 84380 092 6 and was funded by the UK Department for International Development (DFID).
The views expressed, however, are not necessarily those of DFID.

Photographs by Rebecca Scott and Rod Shaw

Published by the
Water, Engineering and Development Centre
Loughborough University UK

WEDC

*People-centred solutions
for sustainable development
since 1971*

For further information, contact:
Rebecca Scott or **Andrew Cotton**

Postal address:
Water, Engineering and Development Centre
Loughborough University
Leicestershire LE11 3TU UK

Email: R.E.Scott@Lboro.ac.uk
              A.P. Cotton@Lboro.ac.uk
Phone: +44 (0)1509 222885
Fax: +44 (0)1509 211079

Loughborough University

Including Labour Standards in the Contract

This guidance note provides an overview of how to introduce appropriate labour standards into contract documents. It introduces the reader to the role of the contract and contract clauses, providing a comparison between the clauses of formal labour standards and those that have been specifically developed to improve the application of labour standards. Consideration is given to costing labour standards and associated benefits.

Further details can be found in *Implementing Labour Standards in Construction – A Sourcebook*. See the Reference section for details.

While responsibility for the contract clauses lies formally with the contractor, the *process* of developing them is best achieved through consultation and contributions from employers, contractors, community groups and labourers alike. Further details on ways to support the implementation and monitoring of labour standards are also included in the accompanying Guidance Note 2: Making Labour Standards Operational.

Conditions of Contract and labour standards

The construction sector is a highly competitive one. Contractors often look for short cuts – especially in areas of lowering labour costs, the employment of a casual labour force, or limited (if any) health and safety provision – to save costs. The Contractor's awareness of certain laws and the need to apply them, may also be limited. This is often exacerbated in situations of informal contracting, where the responsibilities and liabilities of different parties to the contract are not clearly understood and agreed. The combined result in such cases is often minimal worker protection.

Wherever and in whatever way labour standards have an impact, the construction Contract can be used as a mechanism for establishing these standards. Conditions of Contract relating to the application of labour standards influence aspects of the construction work as it is planned and implemented.

Contractual clauses relating to labour standards are present in internationally recognised and widely applied Conditions of Contract. A principal source of relevant clauses for the construction sector is the Federation of Consulting Engineers (Federation Internationale des Ingénieurs-Conseils, or FIDIC) Conditions of Contract for Works of Civil Engineering Construction (4th Edition 1987, reprinted 1992 with amendments). These FIDIC conditions often provide the basis from which other standard conditions are developed.

WEDC

There are also contractual clauses which are locally developed and based on national law. Examples reviewed in this work include Ghana's Ministry of Roads and Transport (for a Bridges for Feeder Roads Project) and India's Public Works Department (in the States of Kerala and Orissa). Typically, these add more detail to what is included in FIDIC clauses, so that they are more locally applicable.

Comparing international and national Contract Clauses

Wages
FIDIC Part II Clause 34(i) covers minimum rates of wages.

- Ghana Clause 34.5 covers the displaying of notices informing workers of their entitlements.

- India Clause M requires the Contractor to pay workers not less than that paid for similar work in the neighbourhood.

Sanitation facilities
FIDIC Part II Clause 34(iv) requires the Contractor to provide sanitation at the accommodation provided for labourers

- Ghana Clause 34.9 requires the Contractor to provide a specific type of latrine.

- India Clause N requires the Contractor to provide "sanitary arrangements" at their own cost.

The Contract document
Each form of contract brings specific considerations and challenges for addressing labour standards. Whichever form of contract is used, the Contract *itself* is instrumental in setting the basis from which labour standards can be implemented and upheld.

A formal Contract is made up of a number of relevant documents, each of which needs to be considered for the effective implementation of labour standards. In order of priority, these documents for a formal contract under FIDIC include:

- The Contract Agreement: the agreement between two parties based on a clear offer by one party and the acceptance of that offer by the other.

- The Letter of Acceptance: the letter by the employer of the tender, forming the contract between the employer and the contractor.

- The Tender: the contractor's priced-up offer for carrying out the works as specified, in accordance with contract provisions and the Letter of Acceptance.

- Part 1 General Conditions: these typically remain unaltered, but can be enhanced through the addition of clauses in Part 2.

- Part 2 Conditions of Particular Application (Special Conditions): clauses specifying conditions that are in addition to the General Conditions and take precedence over them.

- Any other documents forming part of the contract: these are an opportunity to provide more operational details. While contract clauses provide the *intention* of what is to be done in terms of implementing labour standards, additional documents and specifications can identify *how* this to be carried out in practice. Given sufficient information, actions to be taken can be realistically costed by all contractors bidding for the work and more effectively monitored for compliance.

Including labour standards in the contract

Within the contract documentation, existing labour standards can be strengthened as a way to both ensure implementation and demonstrate benefits for workers, contractors and employers alike. Stages to guide this process are:

1. Develop appropriate clauses to include in the Contract
2. Cost labour standards into the Bill of Quantities

1. Develop appropriate clauses
If *formal* contracts are being used, clauses associated with specific labour standards can be added to Part 2 Conditions of Particular Application (Special Conditions), with details of how these clauses are to be put into practice given in supporting documentation.

Clauses need to be appropriate to the context in which they are to be applied. Where relevant national clauses exist, these should be included appropriately. Where it is considered necessary to provide new clauses, it is advisable to take legal advice to ensure that there is no ambiguity between any new clauses and the General Conditions, or clauses already in the Special Conditions.

**Table 1. Specification clauses for putting labour standards into practice:
examples from Ghana**

The Ghana Bridges for Feeder Roads Programme developed Specification Clauses to indicate *how* labour standards were to be put into practice. Clauses covered a range of areas, including those summarized below.

General area	Specific area	Details provided in the Specification clause
Safety	Protective Clothing	A list of protective clothing to be provided per employee (including supervisors) Additional clothing and equipment required for specific tasks
	First Aid kit	A list of contents to be included in a standard first aid kit, with the need to replace items when they are exhausted, or out of date
	Safety Committee	Composition of the Safety Committee, frequency of meetings, standard meeting agenda and reporting procedures
	Emergency procedures for responding to accidents	How site evacuation will take place and contacts with local emergency services in the case of an accident
Record keeping	Use of records	Identify who will keep records, when recording starts, how frequently records are to be presented and inspected
	Employee particulars	Format for recording particulars of each employee, including name, age, sex, social security number, home address, date of employment, union membership, etc.
	Work records	Standard table format for recording the working hours of each employee, including overtime hours and reason for any absence
	Payment records	Standard table format for recording the pay received by each employee, including payments for social security, tax, etc. Each record to be signed by the employee concerned
	Accident records	Standard table format for recording all site accidents, including the accident type, nature of injuries, measures taken, etc.

Additional items were added to the **Bill of Quantities**, to cover the inclusion of such standards within the contract. These included:

- Provision and maintenance of protective clothing, safety equipment and first aid for the use of site employees (sum)
- Replacement of protective clothing, equipment and first aid kit items (provisional sum)
- Keeping employment records (sum)
- Provision of water storage tanks and safe drinking water for all site employees (sum)
- Provision of washing area for local inhabitants (provisional sum)

Table 2. Comparing specific Contract clauses

Labour Standard	Relevant FIDIC Clause	Relevant Clauses from other documents[1]
Working hours: Conditions of work	FIDIC Part I Cl 45.1 states that working at night or on recognized days of rest is not allowed. (This is primarily for the convenience of the supervising Engineer)	*Ghana Cl 34.5* requires the Contractor to display notices informing employees about conditions of work. *Ghana Cl 34.6* requires the Contractor to keep records of time worked, the class of work and wages paid. Records are to be made available for inspection on request. *India Cl M* requires the Contractor to obtain written permission for work on Sundays and Public Holidays, and to grant a weekly paid holiday to labourers. *DFID Cl K* provides for detailed records to include information on hours worked for monitoring purposes.
Health and safety: first aid	FIDIC Part II Cl 34(vi) requires the Contractor to provide first aid equipment	*DFID Cl E* requires the Contractor to supply and maintain appropriate first aid facilities.
Health and safety: procedures	FIDIC Part II Cl 35 covers accident records and reports.	*Ghana Cl 34.17* details the requirements in the event of an accident on site.
Social security regimes		*India Cl W* states that 1% of the cost of construction is to be remitted to the construction workers' welfare fund.

[1] Full details of these clauses from Ghana, India and DFID are contained in Ladbury et al (2003), pages 63-85.

Table 2 provides a few examples of specific clauses used by: the Department of Feeder Roads, Ministry of Roads and Transport, Ghana; the Public Works Department, States of Kerala and Orissa, India; and DFID Interim Guidelines 1999. They are compared with the relevant FIDIC Clauses from Part 1 and Part 2 of the 4th Edition of FIDIC Conditions of Contract.

Community contracting agreements

In cases of ***informal*** contracting, there is no particular reference framework. Labour standards can therefore be addressed by adding conditions and supporting information into any agreements. A few underlying principles apply:

- Agreements should clearly set out contractual relationships and responsibilities. While labour standards can be incorporated as conditions in any type of agreement (including verbal agreements), written agreements are more practicable;

- Where contracts are already in place and being implemented, review the social clauses in them. If they are considered inadequate, a supporting agreement or variation should be negotiated;

- For existing works, labour standards can be more easily introduced during annual reviews, revisions to logframes, revisions to terms of reference and other such "entry points"; and

- In some situations, the best option may be to seek to influence government procedures such that they tackle labour standards. In others, developing voluntary agreement e.g. during a community meeting, will be the best way forward.

2. Costing labour standards

Implementing labour standards involves both direct and indirect financial costs. As far as possible, these should be identified (including costs for training, monitoring visits, etc.), with flexibility built into the budget to allow the contractor to respond to issues as they arise. Examples of direct and indirect costs associated with implementing labour standards are given in Table 3.

Once the general provisions have been agreed, details of *how* they will be put into operation need to be determined through agreement between the employer and contractor.

Table 3. Costs associated with implementing labour standards	
Direct cost	**Indirect cost**
• Protective measures, e.g. clothing, first aid • Providing basic services, such as a water supply and sanitation • Social security • Insurance costs	• Capacity building, consultation, facilitation and promotion costs • Equality opportunity costs • Transactional costs, including dialogue and monitoring

- For example, if the standard *Health and Safety to be assured* is agreed in principle, details are required to identify what clothing is to be provided, who will be responsible for purchasing and paying for that clothing, who will be responsible for storing, issuing and replacing lost or worn-out clothing. [2]

For both formal and informal arrangements, it is essential that agreement is reached on the cost of implementing the relevant standards and who is going to pay.

- The increased costs in *formal contracting* will typically be paid for by the employer through higher bid prices. In due course, contractors familiar with the implications will be more efficient in the application of labour standards and can improve their competitiveness in bidding.

- For *community contracting and voluntary schemes*, costs are typically included in the agreed price to be paid by government (or donors) for the work to be done.

Pricing the inclusion of labour standards in competitive bids must be realistic and clearly identified. Employers and contractors with limited experience should call on technical support to ensure that prices will be adequate to meet the needs.

The inclusion of provisional sums into a contract enables standards to be costed in the Bill of Quantities (BOQ). They are then not subject to competition. This provides a level playing field as Contractors bid for the work.

Pricing mechanisms must be discussed at pre-bid meetings, where potential bidders are informed that inclusion of labour standards will be taken into account as bids are appraised.

Additional issues when pricing community contracts and voluntary work

It is quite common for small-scale infrastructure works to be entrusted to a community group, without a bidding process. Support should be given in such cases to the budgeting and cost control process, so that the employer and community contractor include the necessary costs to cover the labour standards that have been prioritised.[3] This also applies to unwaged voluntary work.

In general:

- Implementing labour standards should be included in the construction project plan budget, as part of the criteria for project approval;

- If the project is already underway without provision for such costs in the budget, it is unlikely that any action will be taken. It may be possible to introduce simple interim measures, such as making small additional funds available to purchase protective clothing/first aid kits, or insurance;

- Investing in an insurance policy may be the only way to protect casual workers in the event of death, physical disablement or expensive medical treatment; and

- If an insurance scheme is required, it may be cost effective to negotiate at a provincial or State level, otherwise the premium will be too high to insure a small number of workers.

How far can you estimate the costs?

The following table is an example of how the costs of introducing labour standards were estimated in a study in Ghana. Some cost items can be estimated, but flexibility needs to be built into the labour standards budget so that there is provision to respond to issues as they arise.

---

[2] A checklist of specific items likely to be associated with different labour standards, plus a table showing the nature of costs associated with each labour standard in a formal contracting context (based on experience from a pilot study in Ghana), is provided in Ladbury et al (2003), pages 86-88 and pages 48-50 respectively.

[3] See also point 3, *Deciding which standards to focus on*, in Guidance Note 2: Making labour standards operational.

1. *Health and safety items.* It is possible to estimate the cost of (a) building latrines and (b) protective clothing. In Ghana, on bridges sites of between 15-20 operatives, the cost of providing general protective clothing (boots, overalls, helmets and gloves) and clothing for specific tasks (raincoat, rubber boots, dust mask, safety goggles and ear defenders) was between 2-3% of project costs.

2. *Stakeholder Workshops:* Also possible to estimate. In Ghana, five residential 2-3 day workshops were held over 3 years, with approximately 30 participants each time. Each workshop cost approximately US $4,000

3. *Development of briefing/training materials* for: (a) engineers, (b) contractors (c) the monitors. Costs will depend on who develops these materials. In Ghana the NGO that helped with implementation and monitoring was commissioned to prepare these materials in collaboration with the relevant government department. The trade union was funded to provide guidelines on international labour standards and rights of workers under Ghana national law.

4. *Training sessions on labour standards for engineers.* Costs depend on the numbers of engineers involved.

5. *Briefing sessions for contractors* at pre-bid meetings and at award. Costs depend on the number of contracts to be let.

6. *Monitoring visits to sites.* Costs include fee days, transport and accommodation costs for members of the monitoring team who would not otherwise make these visits.

7. *Awareness raising for communities.* Costs depend on the geographical spread of the physical works, the number of visits it is decided to make, and the accessibility of communities who will be providing labour.

8. *Impact evaluation study* to assess the impact on livelihoods of workers before completion of the programme. Costs depend on the scope of the study.

Benefits from applying labour standards

Benefits associated with implementing labour standards are potentially available to workers and employers.

Improvements in working conditions support the livelihoods of the workers directly, reducing their vulnerability to various 'shocks' such as unexpected illness, injury or redundancy.

Benefits to workers affect poverty levels and security of livelihoods. These are particularly influenced by application of the substantive labour standards. For example:

- Adequate health and safety measures can protect labourers from time – and therefore wages – lost through injury.

- An end to repeated casualization helps to ensure that wages and legal benefits are met.

- An end to discrimination ensures that skills and capabilities – particularly those of women – are not wasted.

Direct costs to the contractor from incorporating labour standards into the Bill of Quantities (BOQ) can bring savings. For example, the BOQ may specify a sum for the contractor to employ a part-time record keeper on site. This not only assists with monitoring the application of labour standards, but also aids the contractor in managing the workforce, and budgets, more effectively. It may be that an investment in one area brings financial savings to other areas.

Impacts of applying labour standards

In the broader context, the application of labour standards ensures decent working conditions that can increase productivity. Improved conditions and worker health in turn results in a lower turnover of staff, promoting greater cooperation and motivation within the workforce. Such conditions contribute to overall construction productivity, providing the opportunity for a win-win situation for the employer. If done gradually and correctly, application of labour standards improves the lives of employees, so providing benefits to the employer through enhanced prospects for success in well completed work and hence future contract opportunities (Ladbury, 2001).

All this can, in turn, foster the social justice and political stability necessary to promote economic growth and greater private and public investment in the sector.

Information sources

FIDIC (1992), Conditions of Contract; for Works of Civil Engineering Construction (4th Edition 1987, reprinted 1992 with amendments), Geneva, Switzerland

Ladbury, S., Cotton, A. and Jennings, M. (2003), *Implementing Labour Standards in Construction – A sourcebook*, WEDC, Loughborough University
Available to download from:
http://wedc.Lboro.ac.uk/publications/index.htm

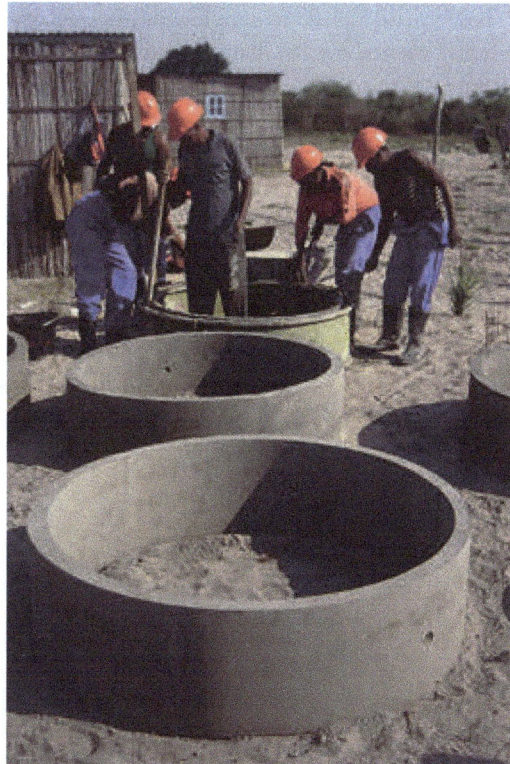

About this Guidance Note

This note provides guidance of how to include labour standards in construction contracts.

It forms part of a series of publications on Implementing Labour Standards in Construction:

A Sourcebook
Briefing Note   :   *Lessons from Pilot Studies*
Guidance Note 1   :   *The International Context and National Implications*
Guidance Note 2   :   *Making Labour Standards Operational*
Guidance Note 3   :   *Including Labour Standards in the Contract*

These are all based on a review of international literature together with lessons learned from pilot studies carried out in Ghana, India and Zambia during a DFID-funded research project.

The project was undertaken by WEDC, Loughborough University, in association with the ILO and DFID

ILO

The International Labour Organization (ILO) is a key organization in "promoting decent work for all", setting standards and creating consensus to sign conventions relating to Labour Standards.
http://www.ilo.org/

DFID

The Department for International Development (DFID) issues paper "Labour standards and poverty reduction" published in May 2004, identifies the contribution that well designed and implemented labour standards can make to poverty reduction.
http://www.dfid.gov.uk/

Website

Further details of the research project, including the Sourcebook, briefing note, guidance notes, papers and powerpoint presentation are available to view and download on the WEDC website:
http://wedc.Lboro.ac.uk/projects/new_projects3.php?id=55

This Guidance Note is part of a series covered by ISBN 1 84380 092 6 and was funded by the UK Department for International Development (DFID).
The views expressed, however, are not necessarily those of DFID.

Photographs by Paul Larcher, Rebecca Scott and Rod Shaw

Published by the
Water, Engineering and Development Centre
Loughborough University UK

WEDC

*People-centred solutions
for sustainable development
since 1971*

For further information, contact:
Rebecca Scott or **Andrew Cotton**

Postal address:
Water, Engineering and Development Centre
Loughborough University
Leicestershire LE11 3TU UK

Email: R.E.Scott@Lboro.ac.uk
            A.P. Cotton@Lboro.ac.uk
Phone: +44 (0)1509 222885
Fax: +44 (0)1509 211079

Loughborough University

www.ingramcontent.com/pod-product-compliance
Lightning Source LLC
Chambersburg PA
CBHW080900030426
42334CB00021B/2618